The Great

Deliverance

By Dr. D. K. Olukoya

MFM Ministries
Lagos, Nigeria.

The Great Deliverance
1st Printing - February, 1998

ISBN 978-2947-37-7
©1998 Mountain of Fire and Miracles Ministries

All Scripture is from the King James Version

Cover illustration: Sister Shade Olukoya

Published by MFM Ministries
13, Olasimbo Street, off Olumo Road, Onike
P.O. Box 2990, Sabo, Yaba,
Tel: 01-868766, Lagos, Nigeria.

Design, type-seting and printing
MFM Press
13, Olasimbo Street, Onike,
Yaba, Lagos.

DELIVERANCE is the act of setting somebody or something free, from every form of bondage. Deliverance is a very important issue, therefore, this message should be taken seriously.

Let me start with an illustration.

An illiterate man took his sick wife to a medical doctor. After consultation, they were given some medicine. The instruction on the bottle stipulated that the medicine should be shaken before taking. But as the man could not read well, he was able to understand only part of the instruction which reads "shake well three times daily", on the bottle. All he then did to his wife was to shake her three times everyday. When he saw that she was not improving, he went back to the doctor and complained. At the second visit the doctor realised that they had not taken the right action. Immediately they did the right thing, the wife got well.

From the above story, we can see that the woman did not get well, until she used the medicine the right way. This can be likened to prayers. You could be praying, without any fruitful result. But when you pray the right prayer and apply it to your situation, something positive will happen.

There are different classes of deliverance, just like there are different classes of healing. The Bible talks about great deliverance, complete deliverance, partial deliverance and instalmental deliverance.

There was a man who obtained instalmental deliverance in the Bible. Jesus, after he had touched his eyes, asked him if he could see. He sincerely answered that he could see men walking like trees, meaning that he was not seeing clearly. Yet Jesus had to give him a second touch before he could see clearly. As that man needed Jesus second touch on him, the same way we all need a second touch of His power in order to stop seeing men like trees.

The greatest deliverance, however, is deliverance from the bondage of sin. Sin is the "food" of all evil spirits. Where there is no sin, no demon can operate. Immediately you cut off the food, they will leave. Sin attracts evil and destroys things.

Therefore, the first step towards experiencing a great deliverance is by subjecting yourself to the divine x-ray or scanning machine of the Almighty. This means that you will let God carry out his scanning on your life.

Some people want a partial deliverance, some want instalmental deliverance and others want a great deliverance. If **you** want a great deliverance, you must fall under the divine scanning machine.

II Corinthians, chapter 13, verse 5 says,

"Examine yourselves, whether ye be in the faith; prove your own selves. Know ye not your own selves, how that Jesus Christ is in you, except ye be reprobates?"

This verse is talking about personal examination under the guidance of the Holy Spirit. 1Corinthians, 11, verse 31, makes this interesting statement.

"For if we would judge ourselves, we should not be judged."

Personal examination is a must for those who are interested in pleasing God and obtaining breakthroughs. It is also important for those who want spiritual revival and a great deliverance. We carry out this check-up because of the constant pollution of the world in which we find ourselves.

A lot of people are very wise with their vehicles, and send them for regular servicing. But they treat their spiritual lives with levity, do not carry out any spiritual check-up on their lives, while their enemies are busy doing what they like with them.

You have to examine yourself, and let the Holy Spirit put you under the divine scanning machine.

Hebrews chapter 11 tells us of people who did a lot of powerful things with their faith. But when you study the Bible closely, you will find that some of those people it lists as heroes of faith may now be in hell fire. Or, what would you say about a man who had billions of dollars and could feed a whole country, but he himself could only eat cracker biscuit and drink milk. He got a deliverance from poverty but not the great deliverance. So you must carry out a spiritual check-up for the following reasons listed below.

REASONS FOR SPIRITUAL CHECK-UP

1. It shows you how much you have allowed God to work in your life.

2. It shows how much you have grown spiritually.

3. It brings to light the dark areas of your life.

4. It reveals any falsehood in your life and locates the areas that need healing and holds them up to the Lord for treatment.

5. It will enable you to receive the medicine for your battered spirit.

6. It will enable you to see any warning or signal of danger in your life.

7. It will enable you to enjoy spiritual health which is very important.

8. It enables you to enjoy spiritual prosperity.

We must subject ourselves to the divine search which pierces into our very depth. The Bible says that the heart of man is desperately wicked, who can know it? It is deep and the only thing that can know it is the word of God.

1Corinthians, chapter 4 verse 5, says:

"Therefore judge nothing before the time, until the Lord comes, who both will bring to light, the hidden things of

darkness and will make manifest the counsels of the hearts and then shall every man have praise of God."

It will expose our need for spiritual surgery. A lot of people don't need healing; what they need is a serious surgery spiritually. When we do this personal check- up, it will expose us to the need divine healing.

.Now, begin to look at your life to see whether there is any darkness hiding anywhere. This will enable you to sharpen your sword, where it has became blunt, because a lot of believers' swords are blunt.

It will enable us to put right some of the wrong things we have done. It will enable us to see our need to offer apologies where necessary. For those who are interested in a great deliverance, personal spiritual check-up is a must. To do this properly, honesty, sincerity and determination are required. You have to be sincere with yourself and your God.

There is something in the cassette player called the pause button; when you press it, it stops the cassette from playing. The television, too, has it, to help the viewer have a closer look at a picture. In the same way, you should put the pause button of the Holy Spirit to every department of your life and hold it there, to see more closely the implications of what you are doing. Wait upon God until He says, okay, you are all right in that area, then go to another area.

A man is basically a spirit, living inside a body and has a soul. When that spirit gets out of the body, the person dies, meaning that all the organs in the body have their spiritual counterparts. If something goes wrong with that spiritual counterpart, it will manifest in the physical.

To every part of the body, there is a spiritual counterpart. This is why it is possible for evil spirits to put sickness in a life and the medical people cannot see it. They attack the spiritual counterpart of that organ.

There is this story of a very rich woman who brought her sick son to the man of

God after she had taken him to many places, both here and abroad without any luck. When they came to the man of God, he looked at her and asked her a simple question: "Madam, what has this boy done to you?" Instead of responding, the woman broke down and started crying. She confessed that she belonged to a witchcraft society and had donated the liver of this only boy she had to her group and that they had eaten it up. Although the medical people said the liver was okay, she knew that her group had eaten it up. We prayed and commanded all those who that ate the liver to gather together, in Jesus' name, and begin to vomit it. That was how the boy got delivered and the mother, too, went for a deliverance to get out of the evil society.

Listed below are the seven things that can happen to the body in the spirit:

1. *Bondage of sin.*

2. *Spiritual chain*: That is when an organ is chained and is limited in use.

3. *Demonisation*: When evil tenants are living in the body.

4. *Evil marks*: The body can have evil marks in the spirit, it can be anti-prosperity marks. Several times while praying for people to receive financial breakthroughs, we have found cobwebs in their hands, which cannot be seen physically, but they are there in the spirit. When the hands are filled with cobwebs, it shows that the enemy had finished his assignment and the hands will never

prosper.

5. *Evil deposit*: Evil deposit is the left-over of evil tenants who have stayed in the body.

6. *Curses*: There could be a curse on any part of the body.

7. *Evil covenant*: A part of the body can be under an evil covenant.

All these things happen in the spirit, but they manifest physically. When you subject every part of your body to be scanned in respect of these seven bondage, then you will see what happens.

Let us consider some parts of the body that can get polluted.

PARTS OF THE BODY THAT CAN GET POLLUTED

1. THE LEG

Isaiah chapter 59, verses 6-8, says,

"Their webs shall not become garments, neither shall they cover themselves with their works: their works are works of iniquity, and the act of violence is in their hands. Their feet run to evil and they make haste to shed innocent blood, their thoughts are thoughts of iniquity; wasting and destruction are in their paths. The way of peace they know not, and there is no judgement in their goings: they have made them crooked paths: whosoever goeth therein shall not know peace."

Think about your legs for a minute. Your legs have stood in so many places in this world. They have taken you to school, markets, and house of God.

Some people's legs have taken them to prison, hospitals, pulpits to preach, classrooms to teach, to work, etc.

Our legs are means of mobility. Ask yourself these questions: "Are there ways in which my legs have run to evil?"

Or as a Christian, pick a simple example: does your motor driving glorify God? After-all, it is your leg that you use for the motor accelerator.

Do you walk about spreading bad news and gossips? The Bible says, "How beautiful are the feet of them that preach the gospel of peace?" How good are your feet as spiritual instruments?

Are those legs walking in the light of God?

Or do you go astray everyday?

To what kind of places do you go?

Are your legs still busy hurrying to where you will be noticed, exalted and acclaimed, instead of fighting to get delivered?

You have to pray today to arrest any power of evil within those legs. A person's legs could be under the influence of the seven things discussed earlier. The only part of the human body that Jesus washed was the feet. Today, allow Jesus to wash your feet . They need to be free.

Please, pray the following prayer points aggressively with your hands laid on your two legs.

1. Holy Ghost, arrest any evil power operating within my legs, in the name of Jesus.

2. My legs, you will not walk away from your prosperity, in the name of Jesus.

3. Lord Jesus, wash my feet today.

4. (Move the hands to your knees) My knees, you will bow to Jesus, in the name of Jesus.

5. (Lay your hands on your stomach and speak to it like this): My stomach, release any satanic poison inside you. in

the name of Jesus.

6   (Lay your hands on your lung) I refuse to breathe in any strange air, in the name of Jesus.

7. I bind every spirit of untimely death, in the name of Jesus.

2. THE HEART

The heart is the seat of all our affections. Love and hate come from the heart. The heart is the seat of our will, discernment, affection and intentions. The Bible says that the heart can be a lot of things; for example, it can be deep, wicked, paranoid, perverse, rebellious, divided, deceitful, secretly enticed, hard, adamant,

21

hateful, blind, wounded, backslidden and slow. It can also be at war within and imagine mischief.

Jesus told some people, "O ye fools, slow of heart to believe all that the prophets have said..." It grieves God when the heart of people departs from Him. And it is almost impossible to find a person whose heart will completely depart from the Lord suddenly. It happens gradually, e.g. when thoughts that should not be entertained come in, they bring in worry, fear, sickness, failure and all kinds of evil things.

When God wants to start working in our lives, He starts from the heart; the same goes for the devil. Where your heart is, will clearly indicate the nature and where about of your treasures. If you are storing all your money in the bank and you are not interested in God's work, it shows where your heart is. Those whose hearts are in heaven, are keeping their savings up there, where there is no worldly bank that can fail.

What is the condition of your heart? What kind of thoughts do you allow? Is your heart pure? If it is not, you had better do something about it now.

Prayer points:

1. Lay your right hand on your chest and pray aggressively like this: Holy Ghost fire, incubate my heart, in the name of Jesus.

2. I release myself from every bondage initiated by bad thoughts, in the name of Jesus.

3. THE BREAST

When strange hands are laid upon the breasts, problems are created. It can result in breast cancer or any kind of disease. It is sometimes nice to cast your mind back, may be to that old man with a big ring fondling your breast. In this way, evil current been passed into people and this is becoming rampant now. Girls in their 20s are now developing breast cancer, because iniquity shall abound, according to the Bible. And this is bringing abundance of sufferings to many people.

Prayer points

If you are a sister, lay your hands on your breasts, and if you are a brother, lay yours in the middle of your chest and pray aggressively like this.

1. I refuse to allow any evil circulation inside my blood stream, in the name of Jesus.

2. Holy Ghost fire, burn within my chest, in the name of Jesus.

3. Transfer your hand to your back and speak aggressively like this: I release my back from any evil load, in the name of Jesus.

4. Transfer your hands to your shoulders and pray like this: My shoulder

will not carry any evil load, in the name of Jesus.

4. THE HANDS

There are sick hands, too. You will notice that the hands and legs of Jesus were the two parts nailed to the cross. We have already prayed about our legs. The hands also need to be delivered. A lot of problems are in the hands, and could be under the seven bondage earlier mentioned.

Somebody was speaking to me in Abuja recently. He said that anywhere he went and anything he touched, broke down and would not work. He added that when he went abroad to study, the enemies attacked his hands so much that any equipment he touched in the laboratory just packed up. He said that it was so bad that even a white man who did not believe in God, called him and advised him to do. something about his hands, as they seemed to be inviting trouble all the time.

Are your hands, for example, crucified or are they polluted? Many hands are under the bondage of blood. Many doctors have bloody hands because they have committed so much murder; killing babies in the womb.

Do you, for example, use your hands to take what does not belong to you? Have you noticed that you have always failed to reap the fruits of your own labour?

Do your hands fail at the edge of a miracle? If the answers are yes, then something is wrong with them.

Please, pray the following prayer points with aggression, and with your two hands on each other.

1. The anointing to prosper, fall upon my hands, in the name of Jesus.

2. I release my hands from any satanic bondage, in the mighty name of Jesus.

5. THE NECK

In the Bible, the neck is always the symbol of pride. Those who are obstinate, strong headed and wilfully disobedient or rebellious. are termed as being "stiff-necked."

Do you belong to this category?

Have you refused to give up a bad habit? Are you arrogant?

Are you like the "daughters of Zion", who go about displaying their necks and every immoral thing?

If you are any of these, you need deliverance.

6. THE THROAT AND VOICE

A harsh voice is usually so because of the temperament of its owner. Your voice can bring people to God or take them to the devil, depending on who you allow to control it.

7. THE TONGUE

The tongue has enormous potential for good and evil. It is so little yet it can cause untold damage. That is why the Psalmist says in Psalm 141 verse 3,

"Set a watch, O Lord before my month, keep the door of my lips."

Do you tell any form of lies?

Do you exaggerate?

Do you distort the truth by concealing information?

Is your tongue a weapon of destruction?

Are you the kind of person who discloses other peoples' secrets?

Or do you have a complaining tongue?

Are you rude in your manner of speech?

•Do you say things that are contrary to the Word of God?

Is your tongue sick? If so, deliver your tongue.

8. THE EYES

The eyes can become sick by what you fix your gaze on. A lot of eyes are addicted to television.

The devil, too, is ready for special TV programmes, because he knows that many

Christians spend a lot of their time watching television and abandoning their spiritual exercise just like they did during the World Cup and many people ended up in deliverance groups.

What do you feed your eyes on?

What do you read? Check these things. Your eyes could require a deliverance.

When some people look at things, the things stop working. Such people need to deliver their eyes.

Many husbands and wives come to me to complain that the only time something work, is when Madam or Oga do not see them. Those eyes need a deliverance.

9. THE EARS

The ear is like a satellite dish collecting information.

What do you listen to?

Are you guilty of being brother or sister "big ears"?

Are you always found where there is any gossip circulating?

10. THE SKIN

All kinds of things have been done to the skin and all kinds of things are happening to the skin.

Great deliverance is when all parts of the body in the spirit receive total freedom from sin, bondage, demonic oppression or possession, evil marks, evil deposits, curses and evil covenants.

Please, pray this last prayer point aggressively:

Let every organ of my body refuse to participate in anything that will dishonour God, in the name of Jesus.

Books in this series

▸Power Against Spiritual Terrorists
▸Deliverance For The Head
▸Wealth Must Change Hands
▸Power Against Coffin Spirits
▸Revoking Evil Decrees
▸Limiting God

To order for the tape of this message
"The Great Deliverance",
write to or call at
MFM Tapes Ministry,
13, Olasimbo Street, Onike, Yaba,
☎ 01-868766 Lagos.

▸Students In The School Of Fear

▸The Vagabond Spirit

▸Power Must Change Hands

▸Breakthrough Prayers For Business Professionals

▸Pray Your Way To Breakthroughs (Third Edition)

▸Spiritual Warfare And The Home

▸Victory Over Satanic Dreams (Second Edition)

▸Personal Spiritual Check-Up

▸Prayers That Bring Miracles (In English, Hausa, Igbo & Yoruba Languages - 1996 Seventy Days Fasting Prayer)

▸"Adura Agbayori" (Yoruba Version of the Second Edition of Pray Your Way To Breakthroughs)

▸How To Obtain Personal Deliverance (Second Edition)

▸Power Against Local Wickedness

▸Brokenness

▸Let God Answer By Fire (1997 Seventy Days Fasting & Prayer Programme In English, French, Hausa, Igbo and Yoruba Languages)

▸Release From Destructive Covenants

Mountain of Fire and Miracles Ministries, is a ministry devoted to the revival of Apostolic Signs, Holy Ghost Fireworks and the unlimited demonstration of the power of God to deliver to the uttermost.

Absolute holiness within and without, as the greatest spiritual insecticide, and a condition for Heaven is taught openly. MFM is a do-it-yourself Gospel Ministry, where your hands are trained to wage war and your fingers to fight.

* Sunday - Worship 7:00 a.m.
* Monday - Spiritual Hospital 5:30 p.m.
* Wednesday - MFM Revival Service 5:30 p.m.
* 1st Saturday of every month -
"Power Must Change Hands" 7:00 a.m.
* 3rd Saturday of every month -
Spinsters' & Bachelors' Meeting 7:00 a.m.
* 3rd Saturday of every month -
Business Fellowship - 10 a.m.

JESUS IS LORD!